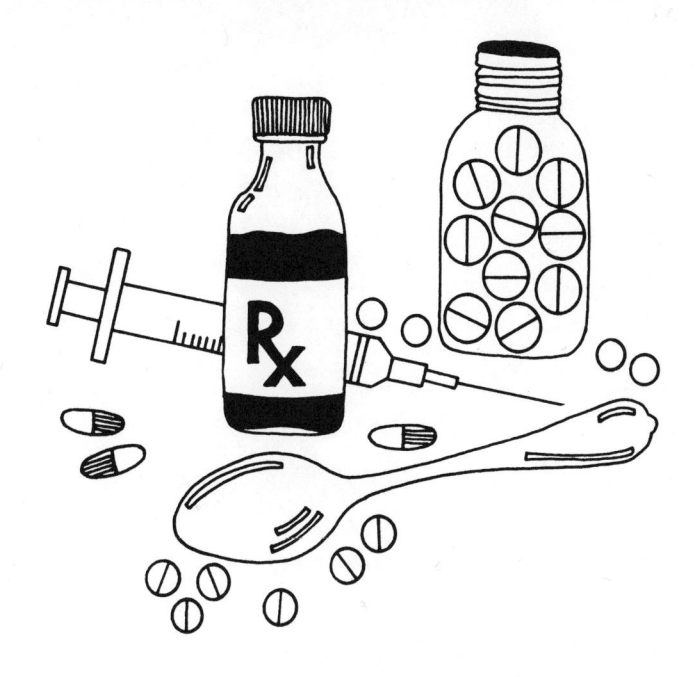

Herbert S. Zim

MEDICINE

illustrated by Judith Hoffman Corwin
William Morrow and Company
New York   1974

The author thanks Martin Liebling, M.D.,
and Daniel Bader, M.D., for their help
and also Chuck Liebling for his valuable criticism.

Copyright © 1974 by Herbert S. Zim
All rights reserved. No part of this book may be reproduced
or utilized in any form or by any means, electronic or mechanical,
including photocopying, recording or by any information storage
and retrieval system, without permission in writing
from the Publisher. Inquiries should be addressed to
William Morrow and Company, Inc.,
105 Madison Ave., New York, N.Y. 10016.
Printed in the United States of America.
  2 3 4 5

Library of Congress Cataloging in Publication Data

Zim, Herbert Spencer, (date)
 Medicine.

 SUMMARY: Defines the various categories of medications
and describes their effects on the body.
 1. Drugs—Juvenile literature. [1. Drugs]
I. Corwin, Judith Hoffman, illus. II. Title.
RS158.Z55 615'.1 74-4299
ISBN 0-688-21786-9
ISBN 0-688-31786-3 (lib. bdg.)

pill

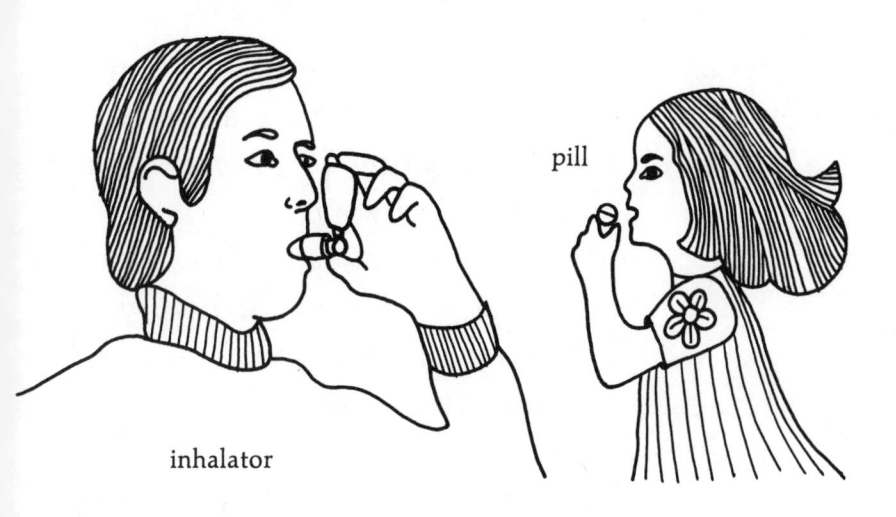

inhalator

Everyone takes medicine. Some take it only once or twice a year. Others need it several times a day to keep alive. Medicine relieves pain, cures diseases, and saves lives. But medicine can also waste money, destroy health, and even cause death. Medicine has always been a boon and a danger. Today thousands of kinds are known, some strong and potent. They cannot be taken for granted.

Though medicines are familiar, it is difficult, almost impossible, to say exactly what a medicine is. Dictionaries are only a limited help. They tell us that medicine is a remedy, a substance used in treating or preventing a disease or illness.

Many things we use, eat, or drink every day also help to prevent disease or help you to get well if you are ill. But would you call water, soap, salt, and sugar medicines? Sometimes they are; most often they are not. Vitamin C in orange juice, as part of a healthy person's breakfast, is not. Vitamin C taken in its pure form to prevent or cure disease may be. No clear line shows us where medicines begin or end. Sometimes a doctor tells us what medicines to take; more often we decide ourselves. Many kinds of medicine are available to anyone.

Doctors often think of the words *drugs* and *medicines* as having the same meaning. Both are helpful materials in the control of disease. We purchase medicines at drugstores. An earlier and more scientific name for them was *pharmacies*. Pharmacology is the study of drugs and medicines.

Medicines are chemicals, some simple, some very complex. We get them from the earth, from plants, from animals, from people. Many medicines once obtained from plants and animals are now manufactured, because they can be built up from common simple chemicals. They can be made in larger amounts and with greater purity than before. Even medicines that still come from plants and animals are purified and so work much better than the natural materials.

The very idea of scientific medicine depends on the fact that the human body contains many thousands of chemicals. Health and disease are largely matters of chemistry. Some chemicals are as simple as salt and water. Others are so complicated that their full chemical names take half a page to write down.

Life itself depends on chemicals and chemical processes. Many illnesses are caused by chemicals made by germs in our bodies. Illnesses also result when our glands or other organs produce too much or too little of the chemicals that are essential to normal health.

When you are ill, you go to a doctor of medicine. To restore your health, he may have you take one or more medicines. Medicines sold in the United States are of two general types. The first are medicines that are usually safe for an adult person as long as he follows instructions. In normal use they are not likely to be dangerous. These over-the-counter drugs are widely advertised and displayed, and they are sold to anyone.

Other medicines can be purchased only if one has a written prescription from a doctor. This prescription tells the druggist how much of the medicine to sell you, how often it is to be taken, and how many times you can purchase the medicine. Prescription medicines are likely to be more potent and more dangerous if misused. Some are habit-forming or have other undesirable effects. Some prescription medicines need to be freshly made. Some lose their strength and a few become dangerous as they age.

Not long ago the prescription told the druggist how to prepare the medicine. It in-

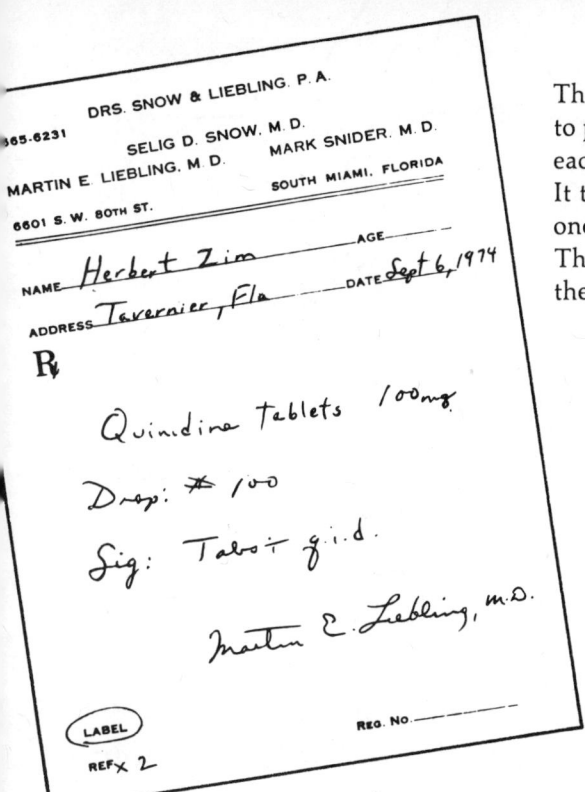

This prescription tells the druggist to put up 100 tablets of quinidine, each containing 100 mg of medicine. It tells the patient to take one tablet four times a day. The bottle is to be labeled and the prescription can be filled twice.

structed him on the ingredients to be used and how they were to be mixed or compounded into pills, powders, or liquids. Nowadays a druggist rarely compounds or mixes medicines. He obtains them already prepared according to strict government standards of purity. His task usually is to count or measure out the drug that the doctor prescribes.

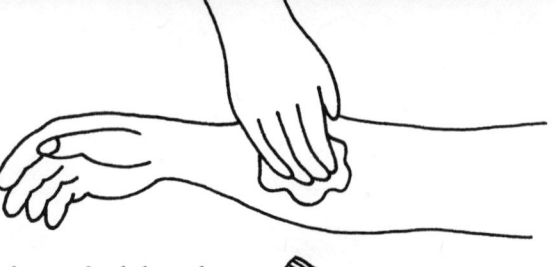

Some medicines can be applied directly to the sick or injured part.

Medicines get into the body in several different ways. Often the path must be specially suited to the illness and the kind of medicine. A few medicines, like those that help to heal a cut or a burn, can be applied directly.

Other medicines are absorbed. They can be rubbed into the skin to relieve sore muscles just below. They can be put into the mouth and held against the inside of the cheek or under the tongue until they are absorbed through the thin membranes. Some medicines may be sprayed into your mouth or nose. You can inhale medicinal vapors into your lungs, and they can be absorbed through most membranes inside the body. If a very sick person cannot swallow or if medicines make him vomit, some can be inserted into the rectum and are absorbed through its membranes.

Another familiar way of taking medicine is by injection. The medicine, in liquid form, is sucked into a syringe (a simple miniature pump) through a sharp, hollow needle. The same needle is used to inject it. Sometimes a special "gun" without a needle does the injecting. Injections are usually given by doctors or nurses. When the treatment of a disease requires frequent injections, a person can learn to give them himself. This procedure is not difficult, and in some countries injections done at home are quite common.

While you may think that injections are all the same, the doctor knows that there are three main types. Medicines can be injected just under the skin. Then they are absorbed through the nearby cells until they enter the blood. Medicines can also be injected deeper into the muscles as in your upper arm or thigh. Then they are absorbed more regularly and rapidly. Finally medicines can be injected directly into the blood at a vein. Then they are absorbed most rapidly. This kind of injection, however, may be dangerous.

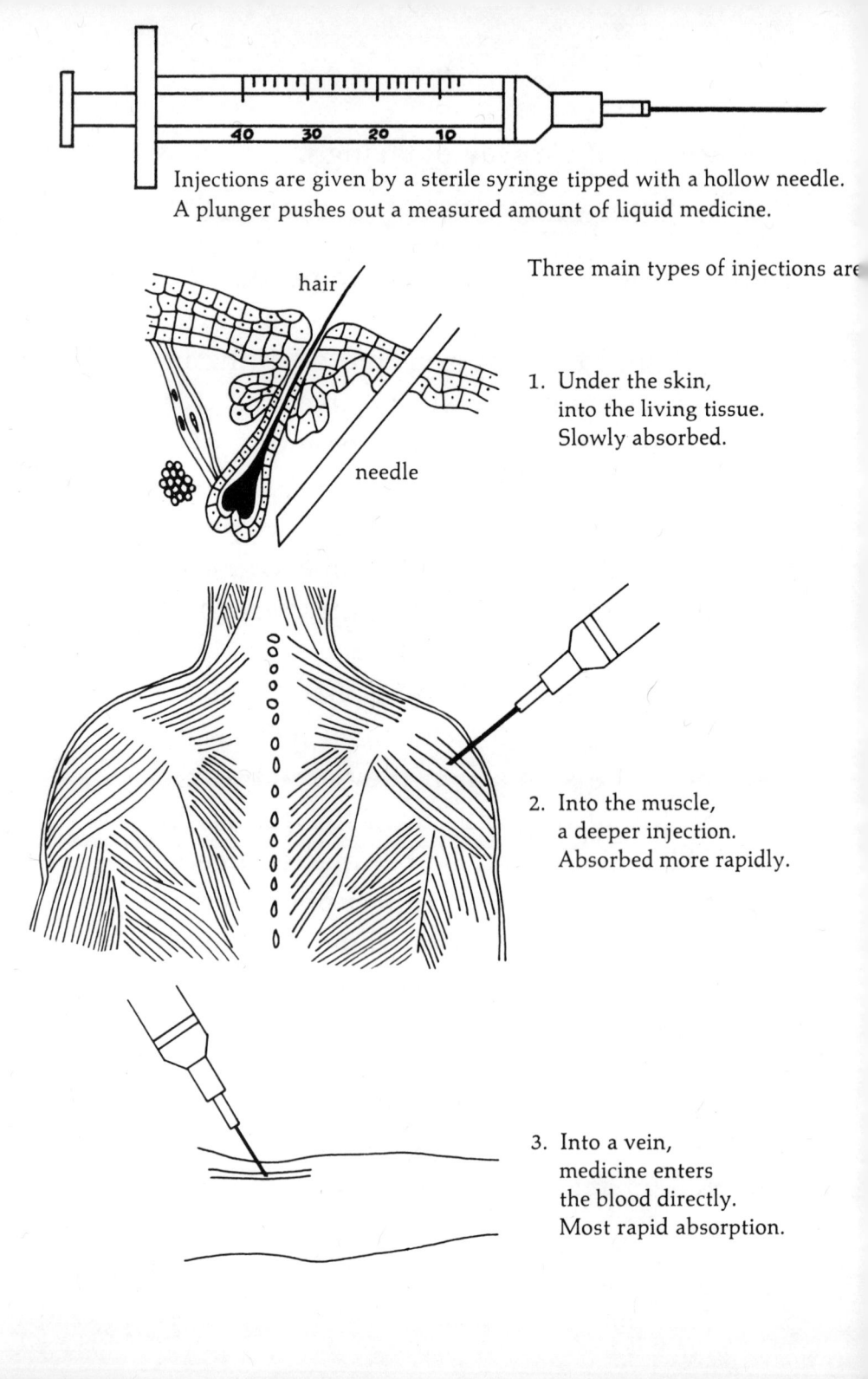

Injections are given by a sterile syringe tipped with a hollow needle. A plunger pushes out a measured amount of liquid medicine.

Three main types of injections are

1. Under the skin, into the living tissue. Slowly absorbed.

2. Into the muscle, a deeper injection. Absorbed more rapidly.

3. Into a vein, medicine enters the blood directly. Most rapid absorption.

Most commonly, medicines are taken by mouth and swallowed. Within a second or so, the medicine as a powder, pill, capsule, or liquid is in your stomach. But from there it has a long path to follow. First the medicine dissolves in the digesting juices. The medicine can sometimes be prepared in a special way to dissolve rapidly or slowly in the stomach. Some are prepared with coatings that dissolve at different rates of speed. After such medicines are swallowed, the coatings dissolve one after another, and the medicine becomes available gradually. So you have the convenience of taking the medicine once or twice a day instead of a half dozen times.

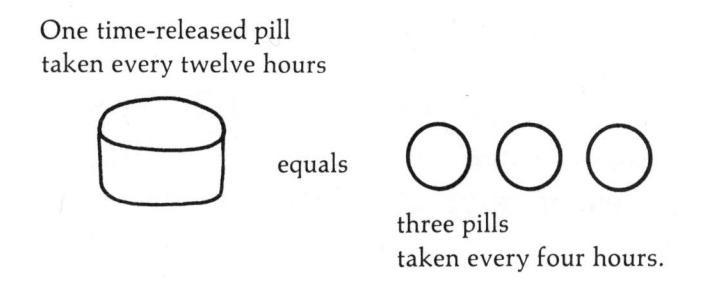

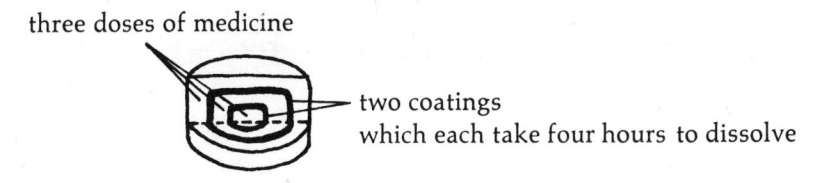

One time-released pill
taken every twelve hours

equals

three pills
taken every four hours.

three doses of medicine

two coatings
which each take four hours to dissolve

Only after it is completely dissolved will medicine pass through the walls of the stomach or intestines. Then it moves through cell after cell until it becomes part of the liquid in your blood. The blood liquid carries the dissolved medicine to all parts of your body.

There is no way in which blood can carry the medicine only to the specific place where it is needed. Medicine for a headache, once in your bloodstream, also goes to your arms and your toes, where it is not needed, as well as to the very small part of your head where it may have some effect. Still, some medicines affect only a specific part of the body, like the heart or kidneys. Even though the blood takes the medicine to all parts of the body, the effect is limited. A medicine that speeds up your heart will not speed up your brain or legs, even though it reaches them.

Sometimes the chemicals of the digesting juices of your stomach may change or destroy the medicine you have swallowed. In those cases you take the medicine by injection or some other way than by mouth.

Once medicines are in your blood, they may not get around promptly to where they are needed. Sometimes part of the medicine is stored in the liver, the fatty tissue, or in other body cells. Doctors know if and when this can happen and allow enough extra, so that the proper amount of medicine will get to where it can be used.

An injected medicine
is absorbed and enters the blood.
It is carried to all parts of the body
even though it can aid
only a particular part.
The large dots show
the path of the medicine
that helps your infected toe.
The small dots show
all the other places in your body
the medicine reaches.

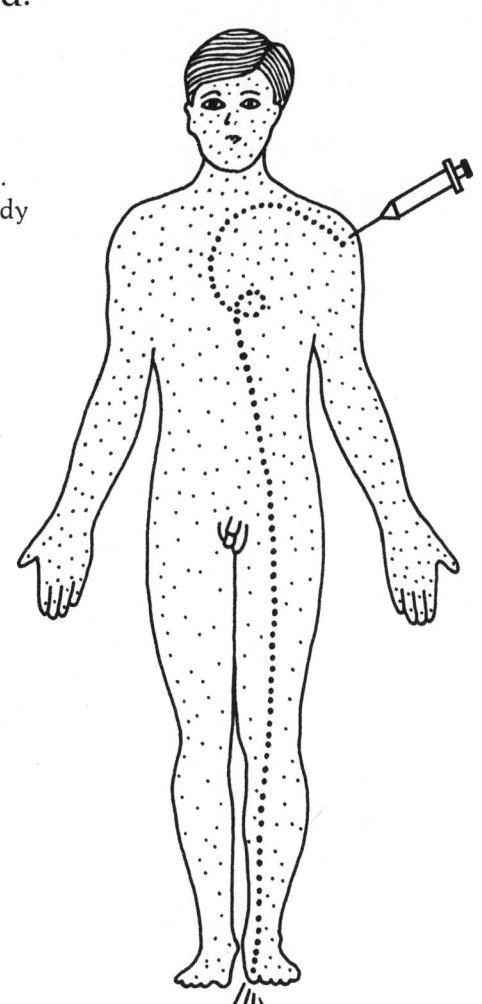

Your body has a wonderful system of controls and balances that keeps all its essential materials available in just the right amounts. Waste and surplus substances are usually eliminated. So is any foreign matter that gets into your body. Even when medicines are the same as chemicals already in your body, they may be in excess of the normal amount. Soon after most medicines are taken, your body automatically begins to get rid of them.

In any case, medicine is used up or changed in the course of its healing work. The excess or broken-down medicine is eliminated and may soon be found in urine, sweat, or feces. The doctor can take a sample of your blood and measure how much of the medicine

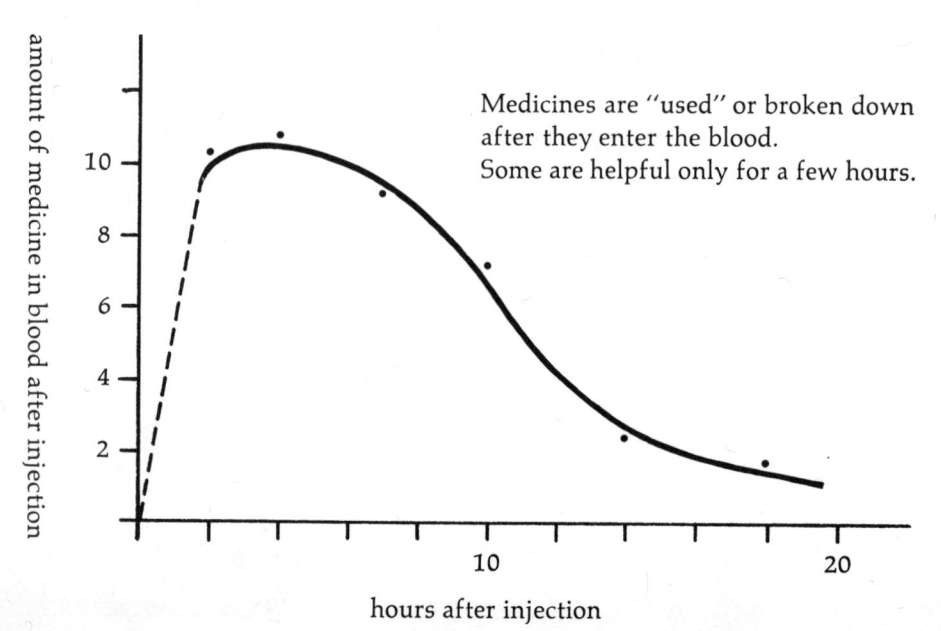

Medicines are "used" or broken down after they enter the blood.
Some are helpful only for a few hours.

is still dissolved in it. Long experiments and studies lie behind your doctor's instruction to take a medicine every four hours or after every meal. To determine the proper dose and timing of a medicine may require as much effort and study as went into the actual discovery of the drug.

The amount of medicine needed has been slowly and carefully worked out. It depends on the illness and also on the chemical nature of the medicine. In a general way, too much of any medicine is dangerous. Some can be taken safely by the spoonful or by the glassful. Others may be in excess if the dose is the size of a pinhead.

The amount of medicine to be taken often depends on the person's size and weight, since the medicine is distributed all over the body. Hence, an infant or small child gets a much smaller dose of medicine for the same illness than does an adult. The amount of medicine given also depends on how fast the medicine is absorbed, how fast it is used, and how fast the body gets rid of it.

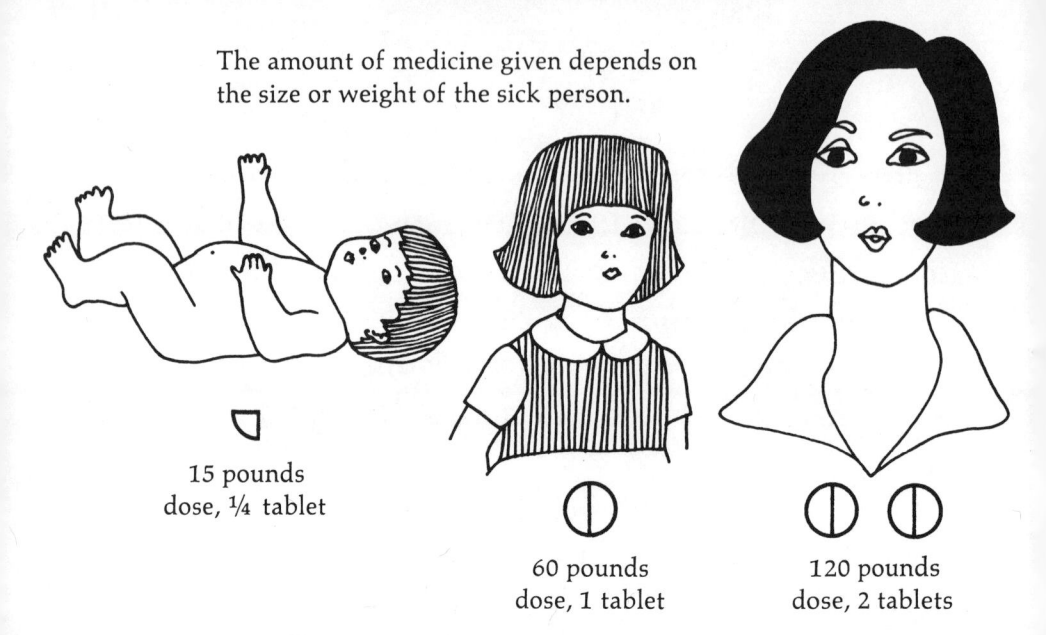

The amount of medicine given depends on the size or weight of the sick person.

15 pounds
dose, ¼ tablet

60 pounds
dose, 1 tablet

120 pounds
dose, 2 tablets

Even with all his knowledge, a doctor may have to work out, over a period of time, the best dose of medicine to give you. For example, your doctor may know that a medicine is rapidly excreted in urine. He might prescribe one tablet every two hours and later have your urine examined to see how much of the medicine is found in it. If the amount in the urine is high, he may conclude that he has prescribed more than your body needs and cut down the dose to one tablet every four hours. If very little is found, he may decide that more medicine is needed.

Too little medicine may not produce the desired effects. Too much medicine can sometimes do serious harm. The belief that if a little medicine helps, more medicine will help more is not at all true. An increased amount may do no good, or it may do harm. An adult with a headache is likely to find that two aspirin tablets will stop the pain. Experiments have shown that a much larger dose does not give any greater relief and may cause illness.

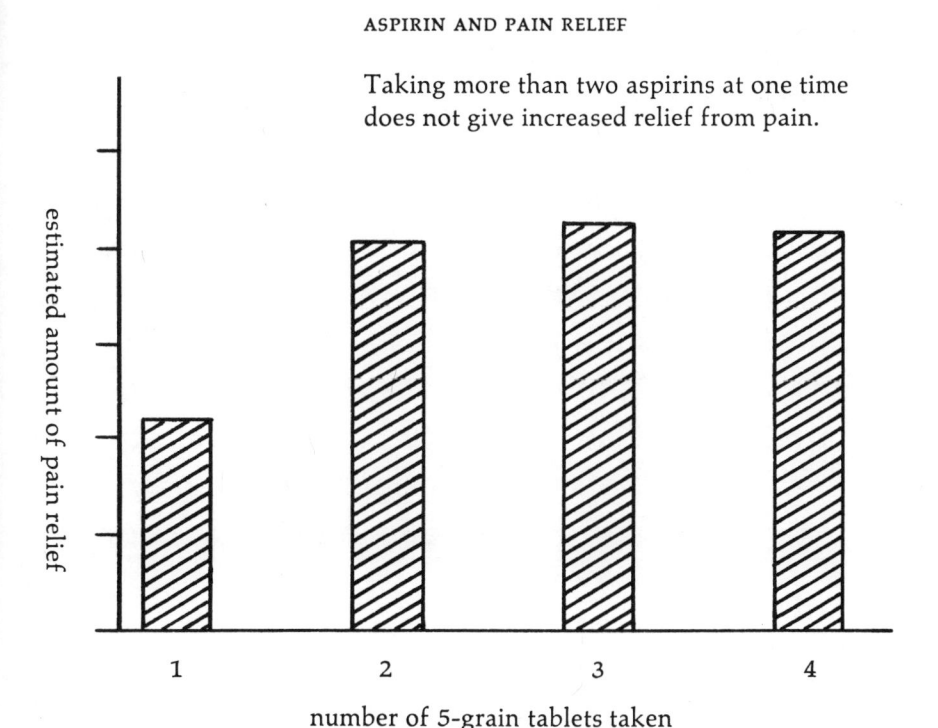

ASPIRIN AND PAIN RELIEF

Taking more than two aspirins at one time does not give increased relief from pain.

estimated amount of pain relief vs. number of 5-grain tablets taken (1, 2, 3, 4)

Men began to treat illness well before the dawn of history, long before other men learned enough to be called physicians. People often believed that sickness or injury was caused by evil spirits or came as a punishment for doing something banned by the gods. In fact, what we presently call the treatment of disease was first a part of religion. Even now people still ask divine help for the sick.

In ancient days, a sick person was carried to a temple or some other sacred place. He brought sweet-smelling plants, incense, or some other offering gift to the gods or spirits, who were asked to help cure his disease or injury.

Later, among the Greeks, Romans, and other people, some men at the temples became more skilled in the arts of healing. At first, these men were priests. Then they were considered physicians, who learned to use plants, animals, and materials from the earth to benefit patients. Through the centuries knowledge grew and skills improved.

Sick people were once taken to temples or shrines to be cured.

One idea, only a few hundred years old, was known as the doctrine of signatures. Physicians believed that many plants or animals contained a sign, or signature, that told those who understood just how the plant or animal could be used in the treatment of disease. A common woodland plant of Europe and North America was called liverwort, because the divided leaf looked like the three divisions of the liver. People believed this signature showed that liverwort could be used for any illness of the liver.

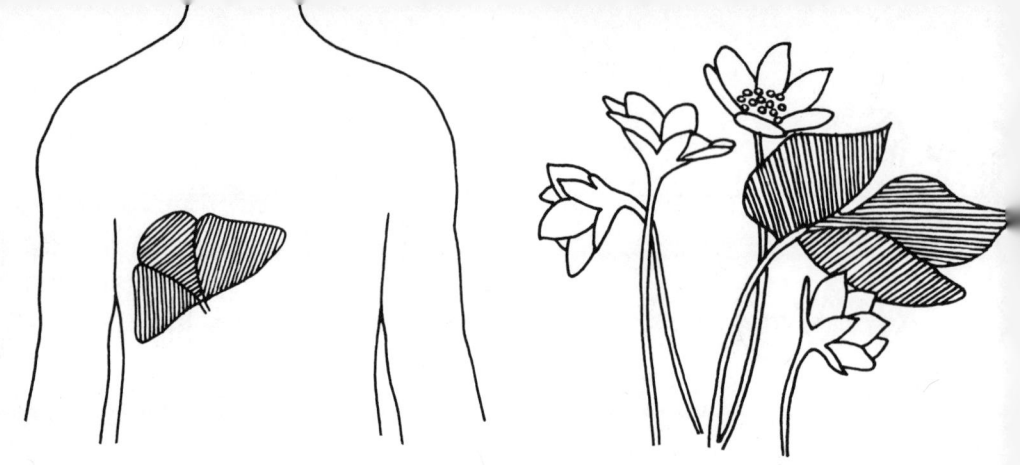

Because the leaf of liverwort looks like the liver, it was long used as medicine.

Hundreds of other plants with signatures were identified. These plants were gathered in woods and fields or were raised in the physician's garden. All were used in medicine. Physicians gradually learned that some were much more effective than others. Such plants became widely known and respected. Today they still provide medicine.

One such plant we know as foxglove, or digitalis, because the flower seems to have the shape of a finger (a digit). Digitalis was used before the year 1200 for a number of diseases including dropsy, a heart condition in which fluids also build up in the body tissues.

About 1800, after centuries of use, doctors discovered that digitalis increased the force by which the heart muscles contract and pump blood. Since then, and even today, digitalis, made from foxglove or as a pure chemical, is prescribed in the treatment of several heart diseases.

Some ancient medicines seem silly or stupid now. For example, the skin of toads, dried and powdered, was once thought to relieve toothache and bleeding gums. Much later scientists learned that the skin of toads does contain a chemical that causes blood vessels to contract. Hence, it can slow down or stop local bleeding. The purified chemical is now used, however, instead of extracting it from the skin of toads.

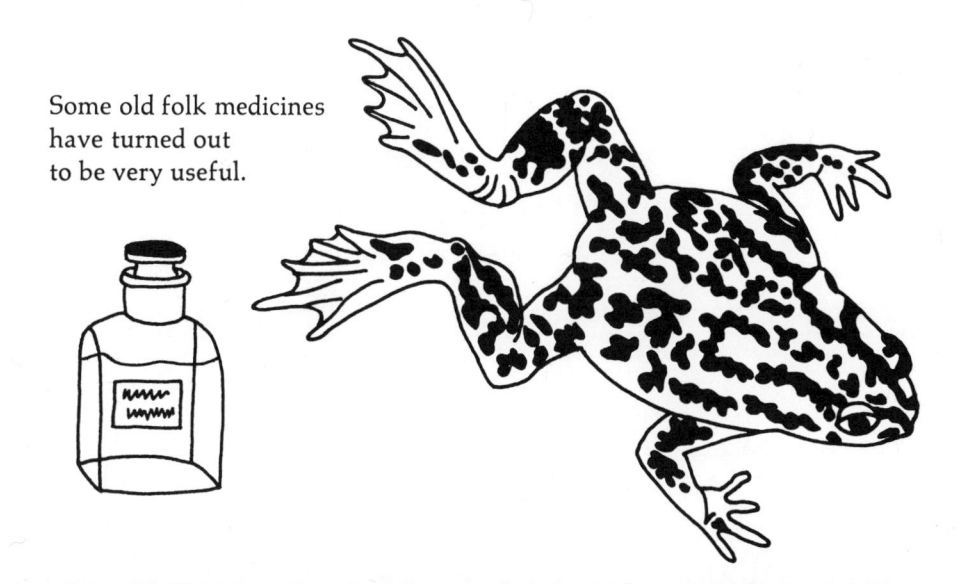

Some old folk medicines have turned out to be very useful.

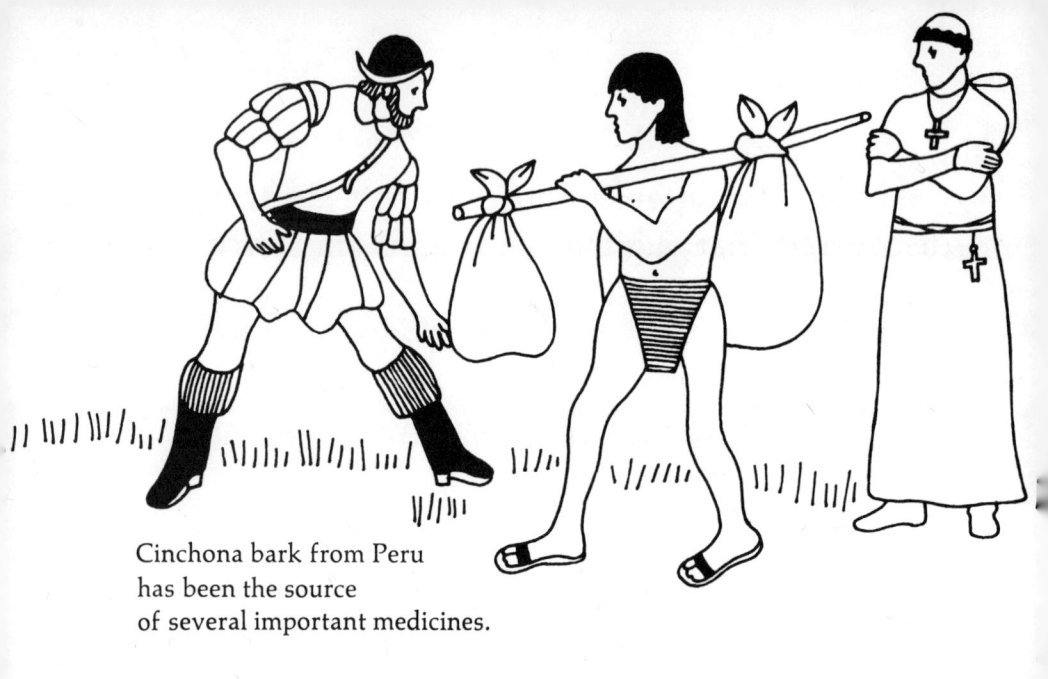

Cinchona bark from Peru
has been the source
of several important medicines.

In the early 1600's, Indians of Peru told the Spaniards about a bitter bark that they used to cure fever. The Spaniards learned to use it too, and by 1640 it was being shipped to Spain. There it seemed most helpful in treating the fever that came with malaria, a serious disease carried by mosquitoes.

During the years that followed, chemists extracted over twenty different chemicals from this bitter bark. One turned out to be quinine, which for a century or more was used in the tropics to prevent or to cure malaria. Recently more effective drugs for ma-

22

laria have been developed, but they are all closely related to quinine.

For a long time, people associated the bitter taste of the Peruvian cinchona bark with beneficial medicine. During the 1600's and 1700's physicians searched for other bitter barks. The bitter bark of the willow tree seemed to have value. During the 1800's it too was used to reduce fevers. Later a chemical isolated from willow bark was developed into the most common medicine of all—aspirin.

Many other plant and animal products long used to treat disease are now known to have little or no medicinal value. Only a few of the old remedies have turned out to be effective. But some were so valuable that many scientists, during the past century, have investigated the medicines of local healers the world over. These substances are studied and tested. From some, new valuable drugs have been made. A medicine from the periwinkle, a common sea snail, is used today to treat leukemia.

common periwinkle,
a source of new drugs

Think about medicines as weapons to protect your health. Like weapons, drugs and medicines are not needed very often, and when they are they must be used with care. For many common minor ailments, if not most, medicines may not be needed. Your body has its own built-in defenses that give you the best kind of day-by-day protection. And when a protective weapon is needed, it should be the right one. A stick might be a fine weapon against a barking dog, but not a spear or a gun. In the same way, simple and relatively safe medicines can solve many health problems. However, some people demand the latest, quickest, and most powerful medicines, even though they may not be the ones that are best for their minor affliction.

Every medicine can be, in a way, a poison. Used improperly or in large amounts, it may be dangerous. Some medicines produce not one effect but several. These additional effects, like dizziness or an upset stomach, may be very undesirable. Some medicines destroy your body's protective cells or affect the heart. A few lifesaving drugs are so dangerous that doctors will only allow them to be used in hospitals where the patient can be watched constantly.

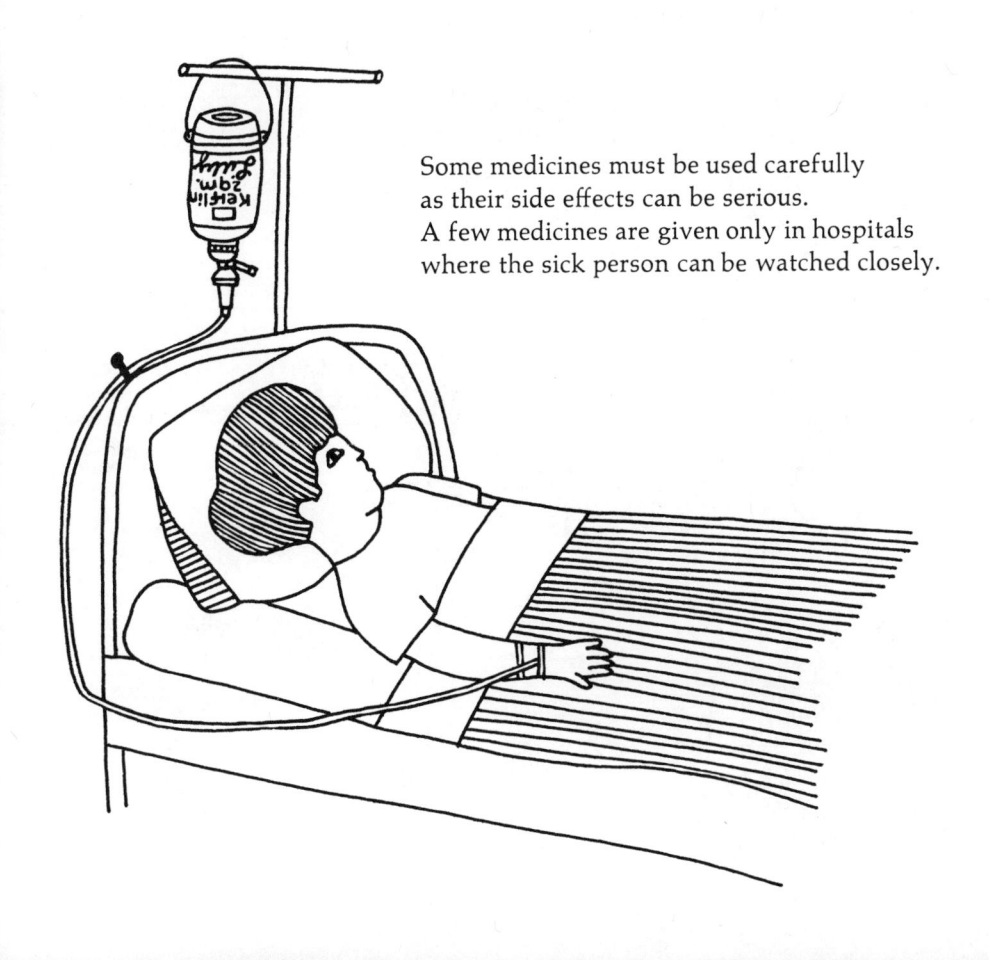

Some medicines must be used carefully as their side effects can be serious.
A few medicines are given only in hospitals where the sick person can be watched closely.

Doctors keep these problems in mind when prescribing medicines. It is not easy for a young person or for the average adult to decide what medicine to take and when to take it. Most people do not need to consult a doctor unless an illness is severe, strange, frightening, or of long duration. Knowing when to stop treating yourself and when to get expert help is difficult.

Within the family, adults often make these decisions for children. Usually they are more experienced, having had their share of cuts, bruises, colds, headaches, and stomach upsets. Sometimes, however, adults are prone to use only those medicines that their parents used for them when *they* were children. Sometimes they may be persuaded solely by a magazine advertisement, a T.V. commercial, or the advice of a neighbor.

Because over-the-counter drugs can be bought by anyone, government standards insist that these drugs be safe. For most people they must have few or no side effects. Anything short of a large overdose is not likely to be serious. Perhaps harm is done when some of these drugs are taken daily for long periods of time, but even this danger may be difficult to prove.

Thousands of experiments may be done on animals before a new drug is tried on people.

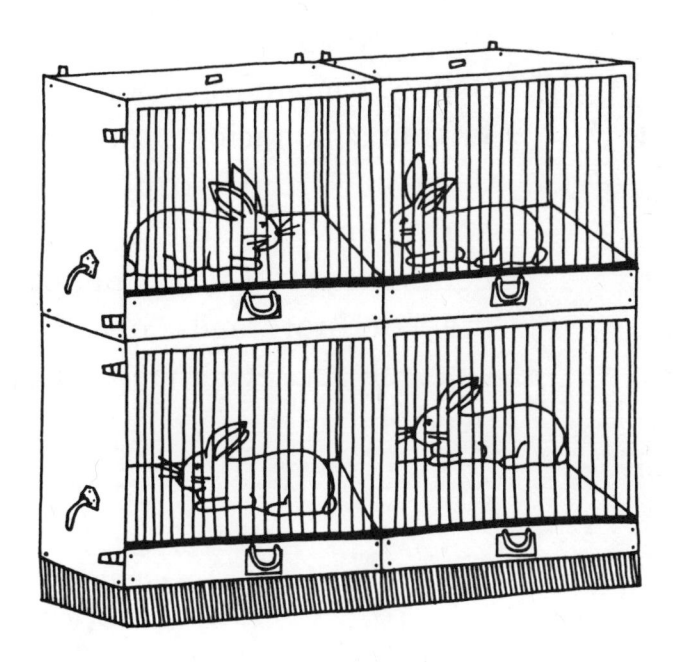

People may use T.V. commercials as a source of medical advice about drugs.

As important as safety is the question of whether these drugs are necessary. Do people need One-a-day Vitamins, Tums, Alka-Seltzer, or any of the hundreds of laxatives, vitamins, antacids, and other preparations? Over-the-counter drugs are not likely to do harm, but they are not likely to do much good either. Why do people take medicines they do not really need? Apparently they sincerely believe that they or their children need them.

People who are in reasonable health often complain about some condition or another. Some adults feel tired or "run down." Young people want to be stronger, more attractive, and peppier. People may worry about a variety of things that may be vague, minor, or not even physical.

All of these people want some change, some improvement. They want to do something about their condition. Taking medicine is one of the easiest things to do. People remember the times that they were sick and the help they got (or thought they got) from medicines. So, even when they are not really sick, when they do not clearly know if anything is wrong, they take medicines.

Doctors know that people do so and that helping a person do something for whatever troubles him is very important. For years doctors have given such patients medicines that they call *placebos*. Placebos may be pills, powders, or liquids. They may taste sweet or bitter. The important thing is that they do not contain anything of real medicinal value.

Placebos do not treat a specific illness, but taking them helps a person feel that something is being done. Their effects are mental.

People who take placebos honestly report, in many cases, that they feel better. Some become enthusiastic over the medicine and recommend it to their friends. Because a person is doing something about whatever bothers him, he feels reassured. Other things that he might do, like exercising, walking, playing a game, changing his diet, resting, starting a hobby, or seeing friends might also make him feel better. But of all these possibilities, taking medicine seems the easiest and is what T.V., radio, magazines, and even our friends tell us to do. Today we take much more medicine than our grandparents did.

Two things are wrong with this choice. Firstly, some people begin to depend on their placebo and feel that they cannot get along without it. Secondly, the temporary relief may cover up something serious, which, in its early stages, is not easy to recognize.

Placebos have an important place in developing and testing medicines. In the tests, placebos are given to some patients, and the medicine to be tested to others. Both look alike, and neither the patient nor the doctor knows which is which. However, a careful record is kept. After the results are in, the doctor learns what effects are due to the placebo and what are due to the new drug.

New medicines are checked against placebos to see if they are really effective.

But the drugs we buy over the counter are not true placebos. Many are semiplacebos; others are safe, simple remedies. They usually have some value for some people. Still, the medicinal effects may be small, and the placebo effects high. People in the United States spend over three billion dollars a year on these drugs, about fifteen dollars a person. Nearly half of this amount goes for medicines to treat coughs and colds and for headaches and other minor pains. Much of the remainder goes for mouthwash, vitamins, and laxatives.

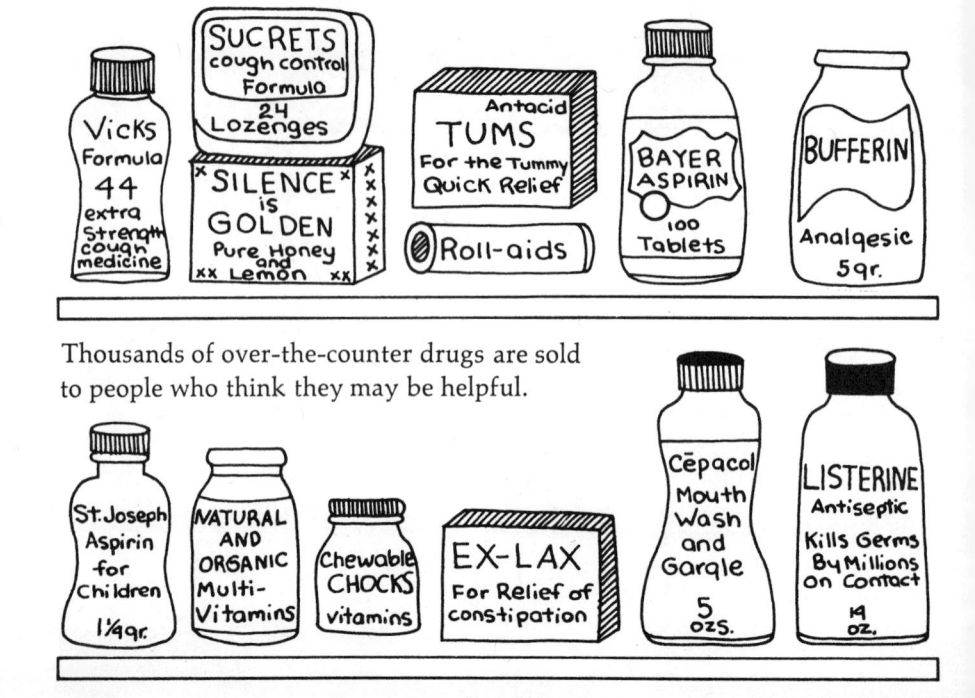

Thousands of over-the-counter drugs are sold to people who think they may be helpful.

The medical effect of these drugs is to relieve discomfort, aches or pains, not to correct the cause. Headaches, nausea, constipation, "gas," or some pains are symptoms. They are not the illness but part of its effects. The causes of the symptoms are often mild and temporary, but may be deep and serious. Many times the causes are not clearly known, but they may be self-correcting. In a few hours the headache is past. In a few days the cold may be over, no matter what medicine you take.

Medicines that treat symptoms do a useful job. They provide temporary relief; they permit you to work or study while your body is doing other things that will get you back to normal health. Since you do not go to a doctor with every ache and pain, only you can judge how much and how often to use medicine that one can buy over the counter. Perhaps the same placebo effect or minor help can be had with a glass of hot lemonade, a cup of tea, or even a quiet half hour in the sun.

A century ago many medicines contained dangerous or habit-forming drugs.

To some degree, everyone must act as his own doctor. Sooner or later each person decides about taking medicines. Our grandfathers and grandmothers had their useless and often harmful "tonics," "blood purifiers," and "pacifiers" for their children. Even the medicines that are of little value are somewhat better today.

Doctors and pharmacists need years to learn about drugs and medicines. Few other people have a chance to gain this knowledge.

The pharmacy is now only a small part of a modern drugstore.

Companies that have medicines to sell tell only a part of the story in their commercials and advertisements. Furthermore, one cannot understand drugs without understanding what they do in the human body. This is the science of medicine. Much is known, but much more remains to be learned.

However, an interested person can learn what the important groups of diseases are and which medicines can prevent and sometimes cure them.

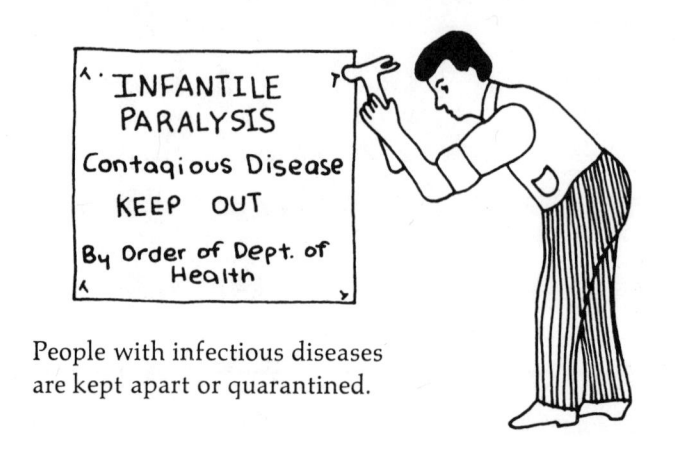

People with infectious diseases are kept apart or quarantined.

One large group of diseases has been for centuries the most serious and most important. It still is in some parts of the world. This group includes the infectious diseases—diseases that are "catching" and spread from one person to another. When serious infections go unchecked, hundreds of thousands may become ill, and thousands may die. This situation is an epidemic.

Epidemics are less likely today, but infectious diseases still exist. Serious infectious diseases include plague, cholera, tuberculosis, malaria, smallpox, influenza, polio, typhoid, and yellow fever. Also "catching" are the common cold and many children's diseases, like chicken pox, measles, scarlet fever, diphtheria, and whooping cough.

Most infectious diseases are caused by bacteria, very small single-celled plants. Protozoa, very small, single-celled animals, are responsible for others. A third group is caused by viruses, the smallest living things. When people speak of germs, they mean any or all of these three causes of disease.

BACTERIA

coccus	bacillus	spirilum
scarlet fever	tuberculosis	epidemic jaundice

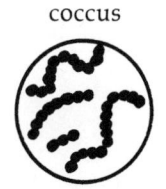

PROTOZOA

trypanosome	amoeba
African sleeping sickness	amoebic dysentery

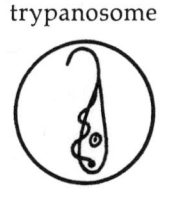

VIRUS

influenza virus	polio virus
influenza	polio

enlarged models

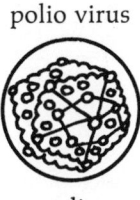

Every human body makes and uses self-protecting chemicals. They work quite well if the disease is not severe. If it is, the body's protection may not be enough. Medicines may be needed to slow down the growth of germs or even destroy them. Germs are killed by many chemicals, but these chemicals also kill the cells of the body and perhaps the patient. The aim is to find chemicals that will do the most harm to germs and the least harm to the sick person. With this help, the body's self-protecting chemicals can work to the best advantage.

One group of useful drugs, called sulfonamides, or sulfa drugs, was developed from dye chemicals. About twenty of them were made from thousands of chemicals tested. These twenty have saved thousands of lives. Some do better against one or another disease, and some must be used with special care as their side effects are dangerous. Recently, some bacteria have become resistant to sulfa drugs. When these cause disease, sulfa drugs may be less helpful.

Even more effective are a group of medicines known as antibiotics. The term refers to complex chemicals made by living things, which stop or slow down the growth of disease germs. Most familiar is penicillin, obtained from a mold with almost the same name. While the discovery was made about fifty years ago, the development of the drug and the methods of making it in large amounts took another decade or more. Now several kinds of penicillin and over a dozen other antibiotics like neomycin, aureomycin, tetracycline, and streptomycin are used. Some can be taken by mouth; others are given by injection.

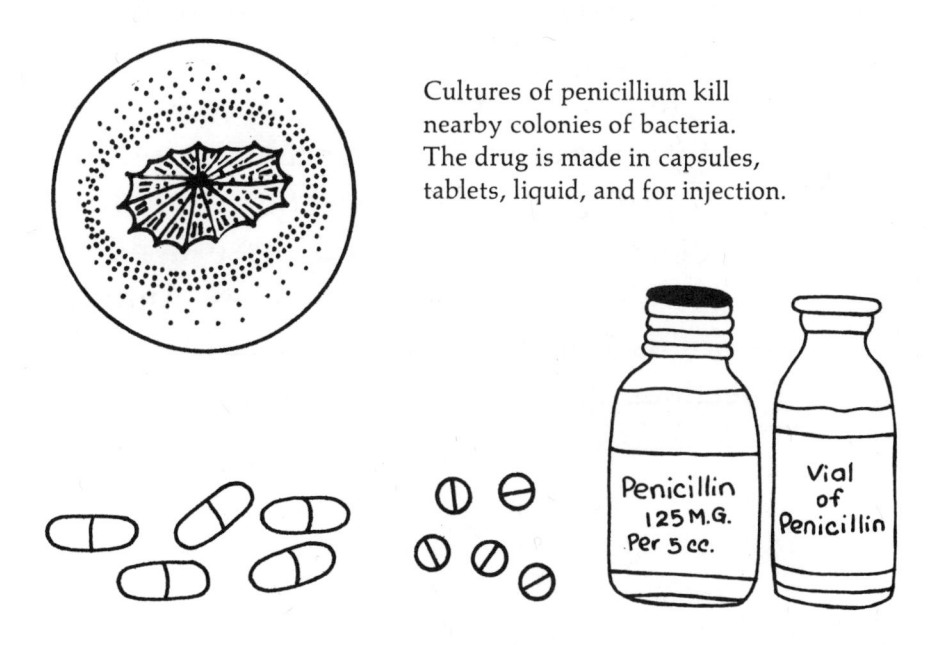

Cultures of penicillium kill nearby colonies of bacteria. The drug is made in capsules, tablets, liquid, and for injection.

Penicillin 125 M.G. Per 5 cc.

Vial of Penicillin

Each antibiotic has special properties. Some are very effective but only against a limited number of germs. They are the narrow-spectrum antibiotics. Broad-spectrum antibiotics can be used for a number of diseases, but they may not be as effective. When a doctor is not sure what germ is involved, he may use broad-spectrum antibiotics.

Antibiotics worked so well at first that they were soon called "miracle drugs." Many people demanded that doctors use these new and powerful drugs for minor illnesses. Doctors prefer to be cautious. Occasionally antibiotics cause severe reactions and even the death of patients. Now bacteria that resist antibiotics have developed, and so some miracle drugs may not be as helpful as they once were.

Antibiotics are still an outstanding and unusual group of medicines. Some are now manufactured directly, and these synthetic antibiotics have special advantages. Antibiotics are used for a number of diseases besides infectious ones. They are also important in treating and preventing diseases of animals.

Another group of illnesses affect the mind, making a person disturbed, excited, or restless. Being excited or restless is not being ill, unless the state of mind affects one's behavior greatly and makes self-control difficult. Drugs known as sedatives have long been used in these cases. They may lessen severe pain and calm someone who is badly upset or disturbed. Sedatives may be very much like drugs that help a person sleep.

Other drugs called tranquilizers are somewhat different. Originally made from a plant, rauwolfia, they help the anxious, tense, or disturbed person without interfering with his normal activities. They may calm someone who is agitated or nervous. Because many people are tense and anxious, these medicines have become common.

A sedative will keep a person quiet and help him to rest.

Nearly all tranquilizers are prescription drugs. Most are used temporarily till the real cause of the difficulty can be remedied. Some tranquilizers have side effects that make a person sleepy, slow his reactions, or limit his judgment. Some sedatives and tranquilizers may be habit-forming. People want them and feel that they must have them, even though the drug is not badly needed. Doctors are concerned that people want such drugs for a quick treatment of conditions that really need to be worked out slowly in a better and more permanent way.

People may also develop the opposite symptoms. Then they become depressed, withdrawn, inactive, or "tired." Many causes for this condition are known. Medicines may be only one part of the help that is needed. A number do help. A messenger chemical, adrenaline, stimulates and arouses the body for action. It can be supplied as medicine. Other medicines, like imipramine, have helped people who are depressed day after day.

Medicines can be used to affect the brain and the central nervous system directly. These delicate key organs are difficult to treat, however, and only a few medicines are safe to use. Some can be very helpful; all must be used with care.

One very common complaint involves the brain and nerves directly. It is pain. Pain tells us that something is wrong. The cause is often as clear as a cut, a bruise, a burn, or a sprain. As the cause is removed or as the part heals, the pain disappears. But doctors can give medicines to lessen the pain at once, whatever the cause or however slow the healing.

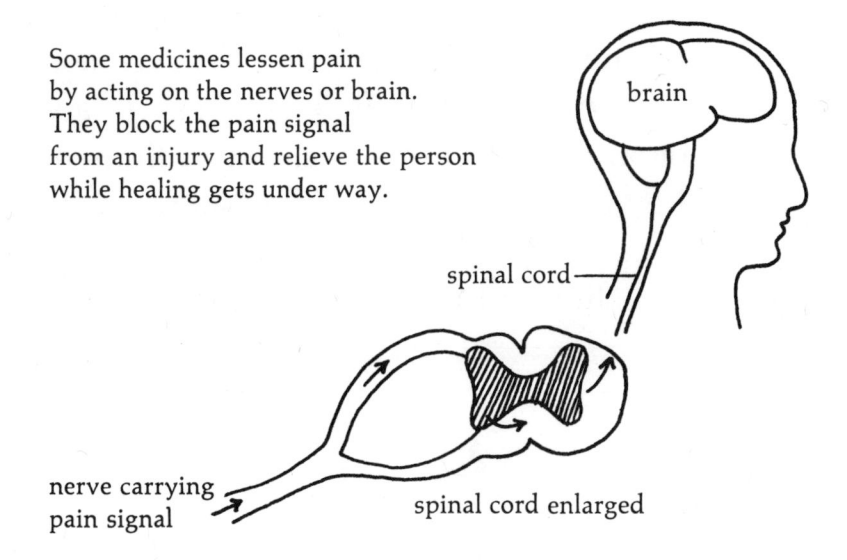

Some medicines lessen pain by acting on the nerves or brain. They block the pain signal from an injury and relieve the person while healing gets under way.

brain

spinal cord

nerve carrying pain signal

spinal cord enlarged

Pain may also have unclear physical or mental causes. Headaches are an example. Most are temporary and soon disappear, but those that persist may be part of a serious illness. Migraine is a severe type of headache that does not have an obvious cause. Other kinds of aches and pains occur in muscles, joints, and in the skin. Relief from pain, no matter what its cause, is something every ill person wants.

An important group of pain-killers are the ones known as anesthetics—chemicals that make operations and other painful treatments bearable. Anesthetics may be the most helpful medicines ever made. General anesthetics cause loss of all feeling including pain. They can be inhaled or given by injection, and they make the person unconscious.

Local anesthetics are applied directly to an injury or, when injected, affect only a limited area. They enable a doctor or dentist to work without causing pain. The patient remains conscious, though the area treated is without feeling.

A more common group of drugs, called analgesics, temporarily stop or reduce pain in less drastic ways. These mild pain-killers leave a person unchanged with all his senses functioning. Most analgesics can be purchased without prescription. They are widely used, and the most popular is aspirin.

Aspirin, manufactured for nearly a century, has become the world's best known drug. In the United States, thirty million pounds are bought each year. That amount is enough for each person in the country to treat about one hundred headaches apiece. Aspirin mixed with other chemicals is also sold under a variety of names. These other chemicals may not be needed by most people.

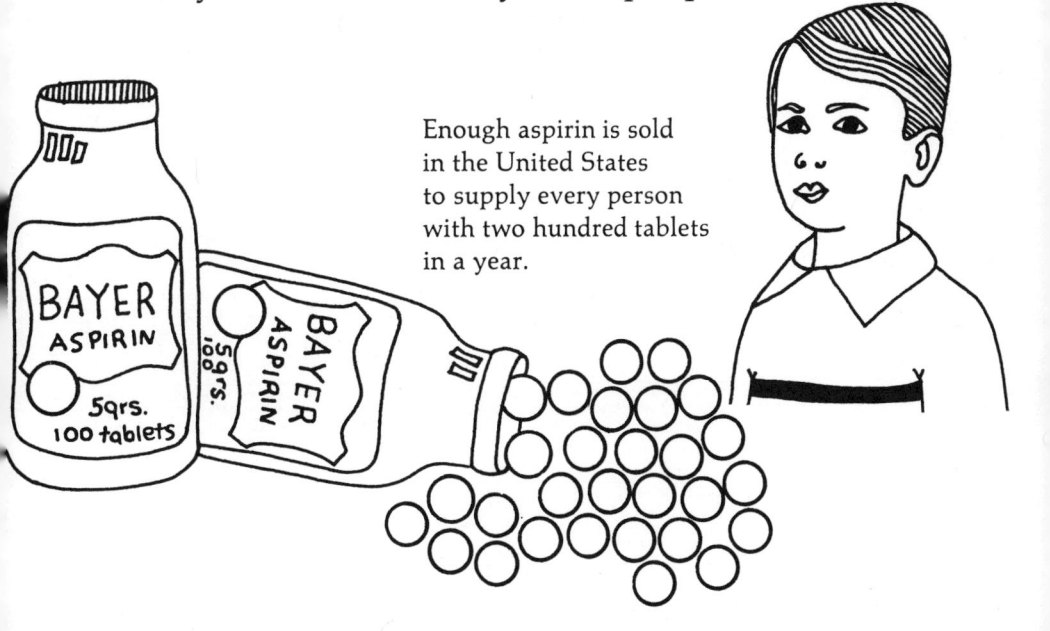

Enough aspirin is sold in the United States to supply every person with two hundred tablets in a year.

Exactly how aspirin works in the body is not clear, but it does work. It is quite safe, yet not completely so. A few people are sensitive to aspirin. Someone who suffers from asthma may not tolerate it either. Large doses interfere with blood clotting, and they may cause stomach bleeding, dizziness, and confusion. Nevertheless, for nearly all people, aspirin is safe and usually effective. Like all drugs, it meets strict government standards of purity. One brand of aspirin is not medically superior to another.

Aspirin is an example of a drug that has several distinct uses. In addition to reducing pain, aspirin also reduces fever. Fever, like pain, is a warning, but once the warning has been noted, both treating the cause and reducing the fever are good things to do. Aspirin is also clearly beneficial in the treatment of arthritis, a disease that affects the joints. It is equally effective for some other conditions too.

These properties of aspirin make it a good medicine to use for colds. Colds bring discomfort, pain, and fever to some degree, and aspirin may relieve all three. But aspirin does not cure a cold. Neither do other cough or cold medicines, most of which have soothing effects. Some will relieve the cough; others will control a running nose. Still, the effect is more of comfort than of curing. For this result we spend about 650 million dollars each year. Since colds are self-limiting, one usually gets better in a week or so, no matter what treatment is used.

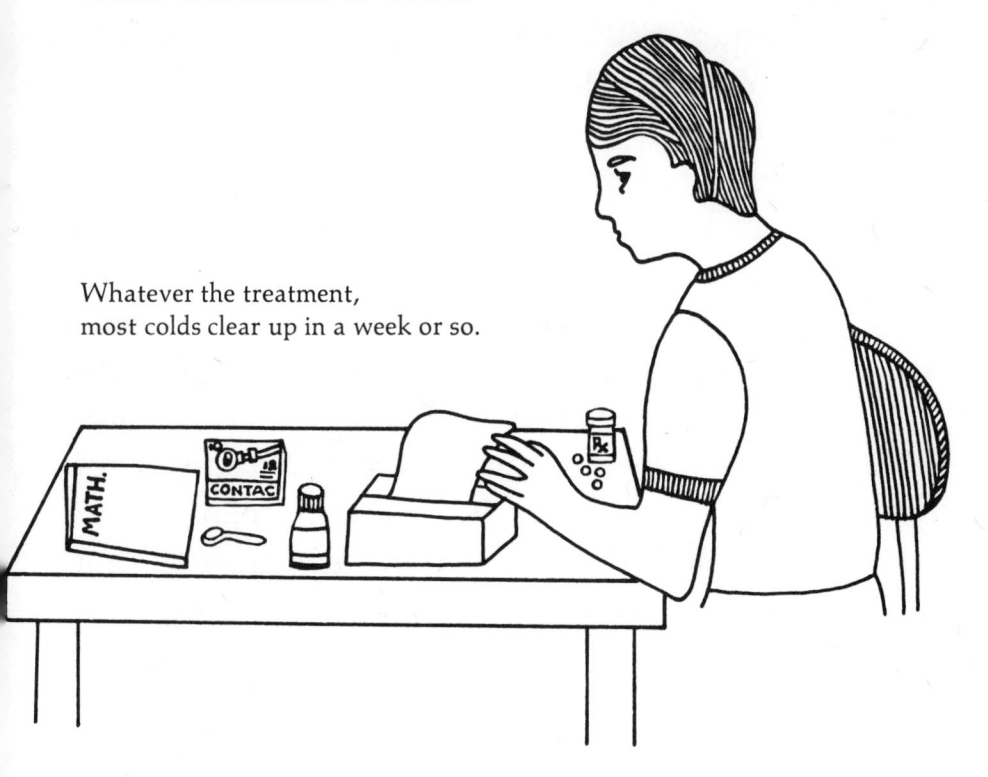

Whatever the treatment,
most colds clear up in a week or so.

Of primary importance are the diseases of the heart. The heart can be overworked as it pumps blood, or it can suffer when its own supply of blood is limited. A number of heart medicines are used for these conditions. Oldest and best known is digitalis, the medicine that first came from the foxglove plant. In addition to helping a weakened heart pump more blood, it also slows down the heart and so makes the beat stronger and slower.

Other medicines, including one related to quinine, do the same thing. Small, regular doses help maintain a slower, steadier, and stronger heartbeat.

Most heart trouble is due to the failure of the heart to get enough blood to bring it food and oxygen and remove wastes. One medicine causes the blood vessels of the heart to relax, and hence more blood can pass through them. This medicine is nitroglycerine, a chemical also used in high explosives. But as a heart medicine it appears in a different form.

Tranquilizers also help people with heart conditions, as excitement puts heavier demands on the heart. Other drugs that prevent clotting may prevent blood clots in heart or brain arteries, where they can be fatal. However, the prevention and control of heart disease demands changes in a person's life-style and diet, not just medicine.

The pumping heart puts pressure on your blood to keep it moving steadily through your body. Blood pressure differs from person to person and slowly increases with age.

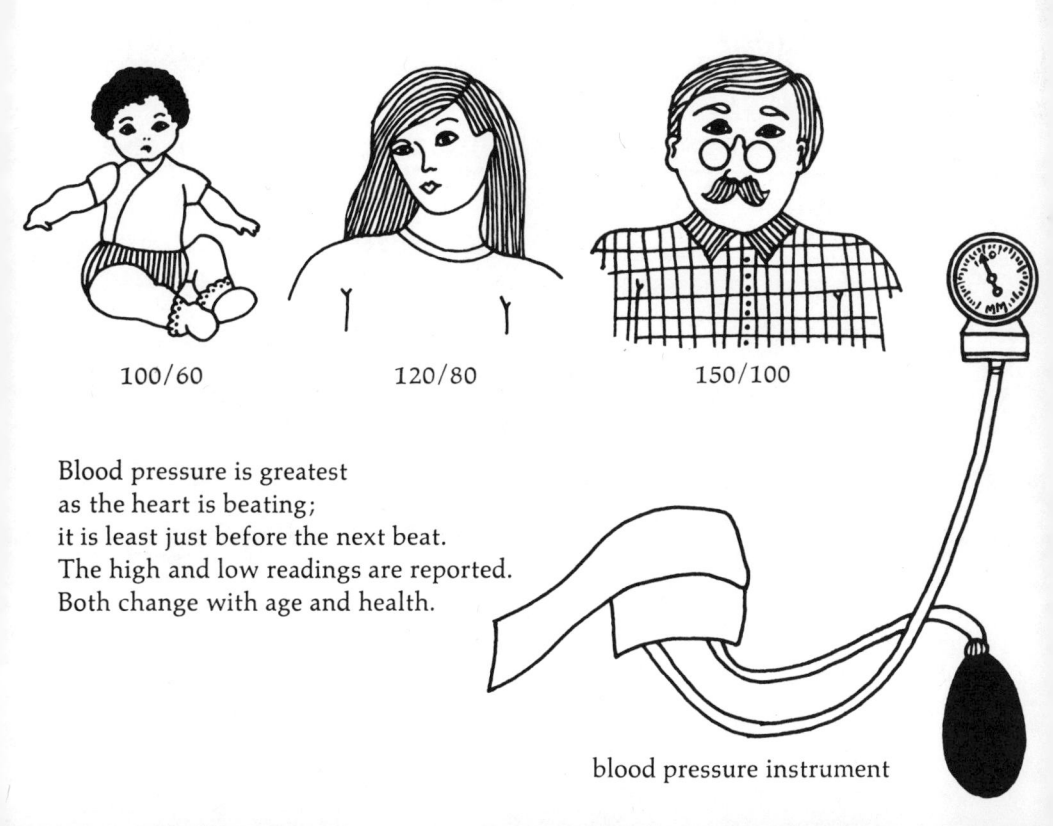

100/60

120/80

150/100

Blood pressure is greatest
as the heart is beating;
it is least just before the next beat.
The high and low readings are reported.
Both change with age and health.

blood pressure instrument

If blood pressure gets too high, it may eventually rupture a blood vessel in the heart or in the brain—both can be fatal. Several drugs, including tranquilizers and those that affect the nerves that in turn control the muscles of blood vessels, are used for high blood pressure.

Increased blood pressure may come about when cholesterol deposits partly block blood vessels. Cholesterol is a chemical made in the liver, but it also comes from some kinds of fatty food. Some drugs help control cholesterol. But more important in preventing and treating high blood pressure is a change in eating habits. Relief from tension and anxiety in business and daily life is important too. So is exercise.

Our digestive systems—stomach and intestines—have minor aches, pains, and disturbances. Many kinds of medicines are sold to treat these conditions. The digestive system may have major diseases also, so the doctor must make sure that the person who complains does not have something serious.

Millions of people have, or think they have, digestive problems. Some of these reflect tension in our hectic lives. Diarrhea, a condition of loose or watery stools, may be due to the actions of germs. Medicines made of purified clay and pectin (from apples) coat and soothe the digestive linings. Some antibiotics or sulfa drugs also help, and finally opium drugs like paregoric slow down the actions that produce diarrhea.

Just the opposite condition is constipation, in which the feces are hard and difficult to pass. In this case, our overattention to being "regular" causes worry and the overuse of laxative drugs. Laxatives are of many types. Some are oils that lubricate the lower digestive tract. Some are chemicals that cause

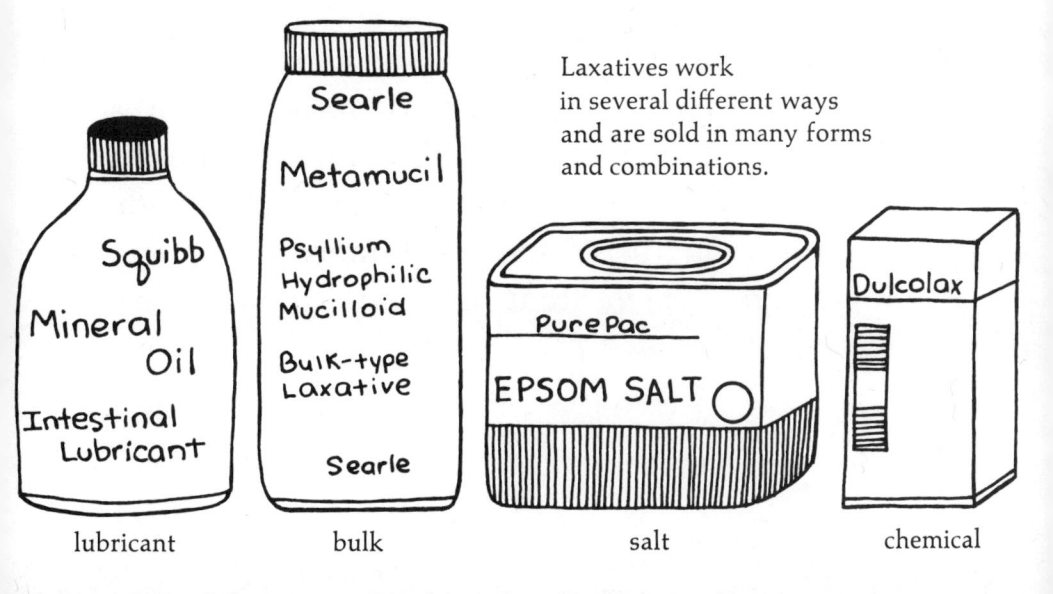

Laxatives work in several different ways and are sold in many forms and combinations.

lubricant   bulk   salt   chemical

water to flow into the intestine instead of moving it out. Some soften the feces; some add bulk. All, in a general way, are habit-forming when used often or regularly. There seems to be little need for continued use of laxatives, except among elderly people.

Another group of digestive complaints come from acid and gases formed during digestion. Both of these actions are normal, but under some conditions the stomach overacts. It may even begin to digest itself. The proper remedy involves much more than medicine, but belladonna (from the nightshade plant) slows down the production of acid and relaxes digestive muscles. Certain other chemicals do the same. Still others block overactive nerves and so help control digestion.

Gas may be due to eating habits or other causes. The same is true of heartburn or a feeling of overeating. A few simple chemicals or mixtures sold under a variety of trade names may be of some assistance. But many doctors believe that they are unnecessary

Hurried eating habits and tension cause some digestive complaints, which disappear when people are more relaxed.

and that reasonable, relaxed eating and living habits are much more important.

Deficiencies in diet are connected with various illnesses. For example, the severe lack of a vitamin causes a specific disease. The cure, of course, is to eat foods that contain the vitamins needed. Lack of vitamin A causes night blindness, and lack of vitamin C produces scurvy. Failure to get vitamin D results in rickets. All these diseases are rare in the United States, because the necessary vitamins are common in everyday foods.

A normal person eating a normal diet should not suffer from lack of vitamins. Today many kinds of foods have vitamins added to them. Flour is "enriched," so are bread and cereals. Vitamin D is added to milk and other dairy foods. Prepared foods often contain extra vitamins. An average American usually gets enough of the 17 or so vitamins that are known, if he eats a variety of foods.

Many common packaged foods are fortified or enriched. Read the detailed labels for this information.

Sometimes unusual conditions produce a disease due to vitamin lack. Then a doctor will suggest proper foods, or he may prescribe vitamins in tablet, capsule, or liquid form. Vitamins taken this way, for this use, are medicines. A physician may also think that infants and old people (both of whom may have limited diets) should take vitamins as a medicine or as a supplement to foods that a person ordinarily eats. If so, he will make a specific suggestion.

Vitamins fall into two large groups. Vitamins that dissolve in water, like vitamins B and C, are the first. When you take in more of these vitamins than your body needs, much of the surplus goes out in your urine. The other group includes vitamins A, D, E, and K, which are soluble in fat. Your body cannot easily get rid of them if it has a surplus and, therefore, has a reserve of these vitamins if needed. But extra large amounts of fat-soluble vitamins, especially when taken by children, can be dangerous. Cases of vitamin poisoning are known.

vitamins
as medicine or
food supplements

vitamins
in natural or
enriched foods

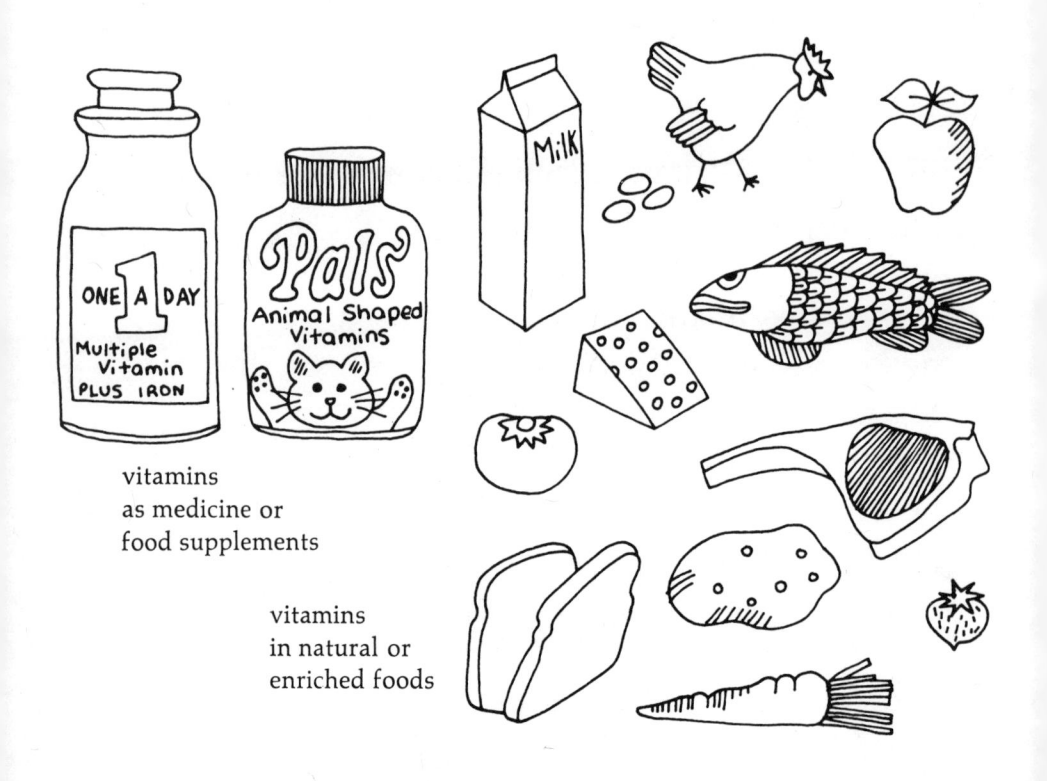

People who think they need vitamins and who buy them as over-the-counter drugs have a choice of over 300 different preparations and combinations. Most preparations contain several vitamins, though there is little chance that a person's diet is that deficient. Americans spend over a billion dollars each year on vitamin preparations, which, by and large, are not needed.

Several illnesses may be caused by the lack of a dozen or more mineral elements that are essential to health. Most are used in small amounts and are so common in food, however, that illness caused by their lack is rare. Your body needs only .00005 gram of iodine daily, an amount so small that a bit of iodine the size of a drop of water is more than a year's supply.

Iron is the best known of the minerals that your body requires. It is essential in your muscles and your blood, although less than five grams is found there. Iron in red blood cells transports oxygen to all of your body. A person whose red blood cells do not have enough iron to do this work has anemia. Over a dozen different causes of anemia are recognized. Lack of iron in food is, at best, only a minor cause.

A complex iron chemical, hemoglobin, carries oxygen to body cells.
Although iron is essential to your life, the amount in a large nail is all you use in a year.

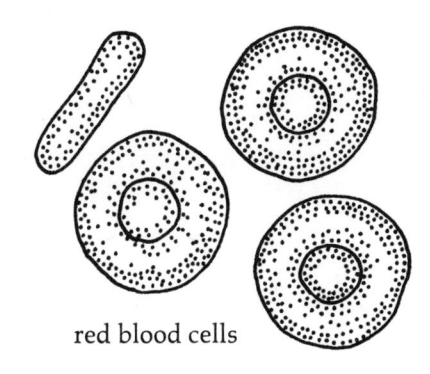

red blood cells

Physicians urge people not to take iron medicines or mixtures of iron and vitamins just because they feel tired, "run down," or think they have "iron-poor blood." Vague feelings of discomfort or fatigue seldom involve the need for iron or vitamins. Yet over a hundred different kinds of iron and iron-vitamin preparations are offered for sale to anyone who believes they will do good.

Health and growth may be impaired if the body does not make the hormones that it needs. Hormones are chemical messengers that aid growth, development, and protective actions in the body. If these potent chemicals are lacking, hormones from cattle (and other animals) or manufactured from other drugs can be used to replace them. There are no good substitutes for hormones.

Even more important are the chemicals that your body builds to resist bacteria or other invaders. These antibodies destroy germs, and the excess antibodies may, from then on, give you protection against the disease. Sometimes the injection of a bit of the poison made by the germ, or the weakened germ itself, is used to start your body making its own antibodies.

The germs or their poisons (toxins) are also injected into a horse in small doses. The horse then makes the antibodies. Some of the horse's blood is taken, and the purified blood liquid, or serum, with antibodies in it is injected to give you protection. These kinds of medicines, which make you immune to disease, are used in vaccinations or immunizations. They are so effective that children the world over (and adults too) receive a variety of protective shots.

Antibodies made by animals may protect people against some diseases.

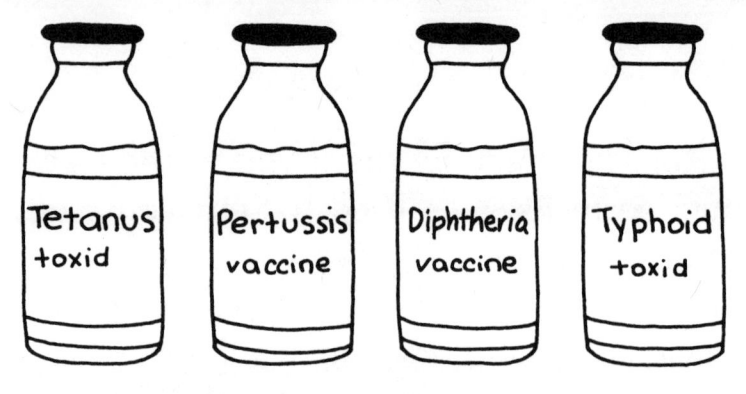

Protection against several serious diseases is provided by "shots."

The use of serums is not without some problems. Under special conditions, people become sensitized, and then another serum injection can be dangerous. People also become sensitized to foods, drinks, dust, and many other materials. These substances may cause severe reactions when touched or taken into the body. Such reactions are called allergies, and medicines like antihistamines are used to control them.

Histamine is a chemical released from injured or irritated cells. It promotes the release of fluids into the tissues and accounts for the running nose of colds and the swelling and sniffles of allergies. Antihistamines act against histamine and so provide relief.

Only a few of the many important kinds of medicines have been noted here. No single book is large enough to describe all known drugs. Many medicines are good; some of the best duplicate chemicals that our bodies normally make and use. No disease exists that medicines cannot help, but there are many that medicines alone cannot cure.

SOME BOOKS ON MEDICINES THAT PHYSICIANS USE

The Pharmacopedia of the United States of America
    This book gives standards of quality,
    purity, and strength of accepted drugs.

The National Formulary
    A widely used reference book about drugs
    and their combinations as used medicinally.

New and Nonofficial Remedies
    A publication listing useful drugs
    which have not yet been accepted officially.

The Merck Index
    A compact encyclopedia of drugs and chemicals,
    mostly used as medicines.

Physicians' Desk Reference
    A book which gives drug and medicine data
    as supplied by the manufacturer.

Current Diagnosis and Treatment
    This book is an example of annual volumes
    reviewing medical practice and medicines.

Many items in daily use can be overused or misused. A number of items are habit-forming as well.

We sometimes forget that everything we take into our bodies has, to a degree, the effect of medicine. Alcohol, coffee, tea, some soft drinks, and tobacco may produce definite reactions. Some stimulate; some depress. All may be dangerous in overdoses. The same is true of many common medicines. The misuse of a number of medicines is the core of the "drug problem." The dangers caused by habit-forming drugs and overdoses of them are indeed serious.

Everyone wants good health, but there is no single way to get it. We are protected by public-health measures. These laws make sure our foods are pure and our drinking water is safe. Such steps toward good health are taken for us. Other things we can do for ourselves: protective "shots," a good choice of foods, enough exercise, and a relaxed pattern of living. Our families and friends contribute to our health also, because love, affection, and stimulation are essential too.

In addition, a good environment is part of good health, and so are working conditions and wages that free people from poverty. Long ago people enjoyed good health without medicines, but millions now enjoy better health because medicines are available. When used cautiously, wisely, and as part of a total plan, medicines help us all.

INDEX
indicates illustrations

Absorption of medicine, 3*, 8*, 11–16, 13*, 14*
Advertisement of medicine, 28*, 32*, 35
Allergies, 60
Ancient medicines, 18–19*, 21*
Anesthetics, 44
Antibiotics, 39*–41, 51*
Application of medicine, 8*
Aspirin, 17*, 23, 45*–47
Blood pressure, 49*–50
Cinchona bark, *see* quinine
Colds, 46–47*
Digestion, 50–53*, 51*
Digitalis, 20–21, 48
Disease carriers, 37
   bacteria, 37*
   protozoa, 37*
   virus, 37*
Dosage, 15–17, 16*
Epidemics, 36
Foxglove, *see* digitalis
Habit-forming foods, 62*
Heart disease, 48–49
   causes, 48
   medicines for: digitalis, 20–21, 48; nitroglycerine, 48; tranquilizers, 49
Histamines, 60
Hormones, 58
Immunization, 59*
Infectious diseases, 36*–37*

Injections, types of, 9–10*, 25*
Iron, 57*–58
Laxatives, 51*–52
Mental illness, 41
Misuses of medicine, 3, 17, 24–25, 27, 62
Old-fashioned remedies, 34*
Over-the-counter drugs, 6, 27–28, 32*, 56*
Placebo, 29–31*, 32*, 33
Prescriptions, 6–7*, 42
Periwinkle, 23–24*
Peruvian Indians, 22*–23
Pharmacology, definition of, 4
Quinine, 22*–23, 48
Reference books on medicine, 61*
Serum, 59*–60*
Signatures, doctrine of, 19
   digitalis, 20–21, 48
   liverwort, 19–20*
Sulfa drugs, 38, 51
Tests of medicines, 26*
Tranquilizers, 41–42, 49, 50
Vaccination, 59*
Vitamins, 53–56*, 58
   as food supplements, 54*–56*
   lack of, 53, 55
   as over-the-counter drugs, 56*